Now do you sort of understand what is going on? I am trying to take you with me to the tormented place I have always gone alone. It may feel like a form of madness, but isn't it absolutely exquisite?

— from the Intermission

# the waiting place

by

## barbara ritter garrison

ACTA Publications

Chicago, Illinois

THE WAITING PLACE

by Barbara Ritter Garrison

Edited by Gregory F. Augustine Pierce

Designed and typeset by Garrison Publications

Artwork by Isz

7/9⁵

ACTA Publications
4848 N. Clark Street, Chicago IL 60640
(800) 397-2282

Library of Congress Catalog Number: 92-074409
ISBN: 0-87946-080-6

Printed in the United States of America
97 96 95 94 93 92   6 5 4 3 2 1

# TABLE OF CONTENTS

This book is dedicated to you:

the lost, the lonely, the afraid.

# I - A VOICE

It came as a voice in the wind, and spoke to me thus:

This is the waiting place.

I hope you have come alone for that is the requirement. There will be no interruptions here; you can think freely and without fear or reservation.

Few come to this place of their own choosing. Whatever your journey, you are here now. Are you brave enough to stay?

Leave right now if you are satisfied with what you know and who you are. When the door closes it will disappear except for the outline in your mind. You will be here forever unless you solve the riddle: "What is Life?"

Solve the riddle, and its answer will become the key to the next place. Fail, and the question itself will bury you. If you have decided to stay, it is time now to begin.

What is your name?

Without hesitation I offered: "My name is Barbara."

## 2 - THE DOOR

Yes, I decided to stay. I have come into the winter
of my life and feel cold and lifeless; abandoned by
the vision once glimpsed, never forgotten, that I
know burns brightly on the other side of that door.

This place in which I now find myself is a familiar
one, for I have been here many times before. This
will be the last. I am less afraid of truth than of
pretense.

I walk confidently to the door, the door that has
for so long sheltered me from that truth. Taking
the knob firmly in hand I twist and pull it toward
me.

It does not open. I try again, this time more
determined, but it yields not a hair in either direction. "... when the door closes it will disappear except
for the outline in your mind. You will be locked in this
place forever unless you can solve the riddle."

Yes, I remember, but I can't solve it this way. I
need to get my books, some paper and pencils, my
favorite thinking chair next to the window. Please
let me out for just an hour or two so I can gather
what I need. I promise I will come back.

Again I take the knob in hand and slowly, apprehensively, pull it toward me. No! I can't believe it. It was true, the door is sealed. I am trapped here forever!

With fists clenched in panic, I pound on the door, crying out for someone to hear and set me free. The only sound returned is the echoing of my shouts, my sobbing, and the pound, pound, pounding on that door.

My hands grow red and swollen. Exhausted, I turn, press my back against the smooth surface, and slide into a heap on the floor. The riddle! I need to solve the riddle, then I will have the key to unlock this passage.

Is there anyone here who can help me? Please, I beg you, help me.

# 3 - SORRY

Sleep falls mercifully upon me.

On waking I notice a trunk fastened to the floor by
cobwebs so fragile they could be broken with a
breath. I pluck at the soft and sticky strands nearest the lock as if playing upon a harp. They let go
and, seeming magnetic, cling to my hands. I shud-
der and wipe them on my dress. My dress? Yes, I
am wearing a beautiful white dress — soft and
luminous and full of little-girl pleats. I don't remember this dress but I do love it. It makes me
feel innocent . . . sweet.

I open the trunk and on tiptoes peek in. Fear and
sadness almost overwhelm me; I want to jump back
but don't. As I reach in, my hands come upon a
box which I bring out into the light. It's a beautiful
new *Sorry* game. No, I don't want this game and
try to put it back, but it has suddenly become so
heavy I can't lift it high enough to get it into the
trunk. What has weighed it down? Oh, yes, now I
recall.

My poor little sister didn't stand a chance with me.
I was four years older and far craftier than she.
For some reason that Christmas we both got
identical *Sorry* games; I guess to eliminate some of
the bickering. I knew Mom's plan wouldn't work

entirely because there was still the issue of whose game would be played when Elena and I were both involved.

Oh, how I had to maneuver and manipulate to make sure it was Elena's game and not mine. Mine, neatly wrapped with cellophane to protect it's precious contents: a beautiful board still smelling like fresh paint, all sorts of little pieces held back by more cellophane to keep them secure in their individual little nests, and cards so slippery they would shoot out like a stream of water. I would never unwrap them, then they would remain forever new, forever wonderful, forever mine. Yes, my game would stay there, beautiful and untouched, on the second shelf of the closet, the left hand side, the side nearest the door — my side, my world, my tabernacle.

"Hey, who wants to play a game of *Sorry?*"

We all did. My heart pounded as I jumped up and ran to the closet to bring out Elena's game. I watched as they ripped off the cellophane, crumpling it up and throwing it into the trash can next to the desk. As each "next thing" was opened, I felt myself grow uneasy at the thought of Elena's game being violated like this and mine on the shelf in the closet, still beautiful and new.

Her game was now open and cards flew every-
where. People laughed as they scampered around
to pick them up. "Boy, I hope I get this one when
the game starts. Maybe I'll just slip it in my pocket
now for safe keeping." Again everyone laughed.
Laughed, can you imagine that? They laughed at her
cards lying all over the floor.

Next they broke into the cardboard pen that held
those magnificent wooden pegs in the brightest of
colors. They were so smooth and shiny it felt as if
they had been waxed a thousand times. Waxed
and never touched, never so much as even
breathed upon. Never anything but beautiful.

I watched those pegs be cupped between two
hands and shook all around — bumping, colliding,
gathering dampness — then held out for everyone
to pick. A mad grab and they all disappeared.
Individual hands now twisted and rubbed off the
shine in the fever of the game about to begin. I was
so glad my pieces were still safe in that closet, safe
from all these hands that would be touching them.

The game began with the sound of the dice hitting
the board and tumbling over and over until a howl
signaled the starting player. The dice were tossed
again, this time followed by the staccato march of
the first player's piece making its trip around the
board. All eyes were riveted on it . . . "one," click,
"two," click, "three," click, "four," click. Again and

again: the dice, the count, the march; the dice, the count, the march.

For an hour all that could be heard were these sounds, broken into periodically by bursts of laughter or an excited whoop or two. That is all anyone could hear . . . except me. Louder than the voices, louder than the dice, louder than the noise of the lively game in progress was the deafening sound of the cellophane, still alive and trying to un-crinkle itself in the trash can next to the desk. I just knew it would get out and chase after me for being so bad. Yes, pretty soon everyone would know. Would anyone still like me, trust me, want me around?

Elena deserved a better sister than I. She was younger, smaller, more innocent, and she relied on me for companionship in those early years of childhood restrictions. She trusted me and I tricked her time after time after time because I was so worried about myself and so capable of fooling everyone.

I never felt good about what I accomplished, however, only momentarily relieved. Shame and fear of discovery would then overcome me. Those ugly feelings never stopped me from doing it again though. It seemed as if I couldn't help myself . . . and, sometimes, still can't.

You must get rid of that closet for it is not
a tabernacle but a tomb.  It represents
childhood's needs both met and unmet, and
means death for the person you want to
become.  Create no more hiding places.
Make of your heart a generous place where
others can laugh, live, play, and find shelter
from life's storms.

Yes, yes, I will, I will, for I no longer want to store
my precious life in a dark closet where it will
remain safe and never touched.

Come, come now all of you, share in my treasures.
Let my ears resound with the joyful noises of life
and laughter and the sound of cellophane, lots and
lots of cellophane crinkling and filling the air with
its song. Yes, come now, I beg you, please come.
My joy is abounding.

No one came.  The moment remained empty and
still.

## 4 - THE BEAST

Time passes and I grow hungry.

The hunger takes me back in reverie to my childhood table where we are sitting awaiting Grandma's
wonderful dinner. Grandma was a good cook. I
don't know which feeling was better, the one of
being full or the one of anticipation borne on the
aromas that would come from her kitchen for
hours preceding the meal: the spicy smell of cinna-
mon coming from the apple pie with the crisp and
salty crust; the onions being readied for their
marriage with any number of other ingredients to
make her magnificent soups and stews; the yeasty
breads baked every other day. Oh yes, Grandma
was a very good cook.

We are sitting in our usual places around the table,
six of us, with our bellies growling out for the
wonderful things soon to come from her kitchen.
Grandma appears in the doorway holding a plate of
potato pancakes, the topmost one still sizzling and
steaming. Potato pancakes are one of our favorites.
She hands the plate to Grandpa, who is sitting at
the head of the table, a place she reserves for him.
He takes two from the top, pauses, takes another,
then passes the plate.

Grandma has disappeared into the warm kitchen to
bring forth her next offering: golden brown, crispy-

on-the-outside, juicy-on-the-inside, breaded pork
chops — six of them, each one a vision of perfection. Not a crumb has fallen off onto the plate.
They are like a picture from a magazine . . . no,
better than that because their smell has now filled
the room and we finger our silverware in anticipation. Soon. Soon the platter will be empty and the
vision will move onto our plates.

I watch Grandpa take the platter from Grandma
and make his selection, the one of the six that
pleases him most. Then with horror I see him
again lift his fork and circle the plate to make still
another selection. No! Can't you see there are
only six of them and count: one, two, three, four,
five, six — there are six of us. No, Grandpa!

His second chop balances slightly to the left but on
top of the first, and next to the stack of potato
pancakes. As young as I am, I realize someone will
go without. I fear it will be me, since I am sitting in
the sixth position at the table. Will no one speak
out to stop this man?

Nothing is said however, and the plate is passed
slowly now, with everyone taking a just portion
and averting the glance of the next person to take
the platter. No one offers recognition of the
crime that has just taken place. Silence reigns.
Thick and heavy silence. I want to scream
"Grandpa you are a pig and you have stolen

someone's food" . . . but I dare not speak out or I will be asked to leave this table, hungry.

The platter comes to me with one chop on it. I look around at the others' plates. Grandma's is empty. She has been serving us and not at the table to take portions for her meal. Now it will be I who is forced to take Grandma's food, for I am too hungry to sacrifice.

When the meal is over, Grandpa's plate is still almost filled with the abundance he has taken. He leans over and says to Grandma, "Mama, I'm too full. Wrap it up and I'll eat it later."

Now and later; then and now; yesterday, today and tomorrow; past, present and future. They all belong to him, and to all those like him who are never satisfied, always wanting more than their share.

Because of their greed there are those who must go without. Our earth is plentiful and generous, able to take care of all its guests, but not when some of those guests cannot live on their just portion, reach for more and more, stuffing it into lives too small to consume it all. They hoard for the future, worrying about their "laters" when some have died in the hunger of their "now."

Yes, Grandpa, I can almost see you — your plate so heavy with food you can't lift it onto the final-gathering table. I bet there is no "Grandma" there to help you in your greed; securing respect for your selfish ways; making it all right for you to be a pig. You did not belong at our table, the table of our family, because you thought only of yourself. You took your paycheck and spent it on whiskey instead of caring for the children you ushered into this world. You were selfish and greedy from the start, and you never changed. I was forced to respect you with my silence, but inside of me, where it mattered, I cursed you and your ways.

Grandma made me dance before you with open hands to receive my nickle on payday. Dance and smile and chant "payday treat, payday treat" because she wanted you to feel beneficent and kindly. But I didn't see you as that because I knew most of your payday treats were spent on yourself and the rest was fought for in a tug-of-war between you and Grandma . . . as if you had a right to your pay.

Your children supported *you*, Grandpa, the father who took food from their mouths. The father who was so jealous when his children got anything he would fly into a rage against their mother for spoiling them. *"Spoiling"* them? Those children scrubbed halls to pay the rent; carried coal and oil up four flights of stairs to fill the stoves; went out in the middle of the night to drag their father home; and then obediently handed over their pay envelopes without even looking inside because it was demanded of them.

And what was demanded of you? Nothing you would comply with. You took and took and took but never gave anything in return. Yes, Grandma clapped her hands and we danced for you, Grandpa. But no more.

Years away from that table, I tell the story and still feel disgust. I see you in people I meet every day who let their selfishness rob the world of justice and harmony. People who, in their piles of abundance wrapped up for later, have that which belongs to those who go hungry day after day.

As I sat at that table in wide-eyed horror, I saw the Beast. And when no one chased it away, it possessed me because I was small and defenseless, unable to understand or fight it off. Now it is I who wants to take two instead of one; who needs to be first to the table; who wants more than she needs; who hoards and hides for later. The demon now lives within me.

Grandpa, I know you are outside that door because I can smell the years of food that have gone rotten around you. If the door would suddenly fling open and I saw you sitting at a banquet table, I would not budge from my hunger to join you. And if you asked to be with me now, I would refuse you entry — choosing to be alone forever rather than invite you in. I will die before I forgive you.

# 5 - LESSONS

All during our school years, my mother worked in the rectory. She would bring home stories of the priests' larder filled with steaks and chops and roasts. Their vacations were to exotic, faraway places, and they had a weekly poker game where the kitty was sometimes higher than the little salary they paid Mom, a widow with two small children.

The message put forth from the pulpit, however, was clear : "No one should have an abundance when there are those in need." They called it justice and said giving from your abundance, even to the point of creating your own need, was a work of mercy. This was not an easy way to live, so the lessons had to start early by having kids give up their candy money to help the poor. The mission can would be passed up and down the aisle each Friday for us to contribute what we had saved by doing "without" during the week. I participated in this practice. My mother, however, lived the message.

Brandt's Shoe Store — what a wonderful place. The experience of getting new shoes was better than Christmas. The almost-best part was outside, where Mom and I would stand and window-shop. At this point, everything was a possibility. I looked at the very high heels but knew it would be years before they could ever be mine. For now, I would have to be content with "flats." That was just fine with me because there were some that made me drool: patent leather ones with bows covering almost the entire front, semi-grown up ones that actually had a sling strap in the back, suede ones that changed color if you brushed them, and regular leather shoes in an assortment of splendid colors.

After peering through the window (faces pressed against the glass to see past our reflection), pointing and talking about this one or maybe that one, we were ready to go inside. A tinkling little bell announced our visit. *Come, come, Mr. Brandt, we have arrived and wish to purchase one of your finest pairs of shoes. Hurry, please hurry.*

Once through the preliminary ritual of taking off my right shoe and having me stand on the metal ruler with the stationary heel and sliding toe, Mr. Brandt would announce my size then ask what he could show me today. Sometimes there was disappointment when I learned that the shoe I had my heart set on did not come in my size, but then Mr. Brandt would suggest others he "just got in" that might be *exactly* what I was looking for.

He would disappear through the curtains into the back room and return carrying a stack of boxes. I felt like running to him and tearing those boxes out of his hands, but I forced myself to sit — even if only on the edge of my seat — and let him come to me. The next procedures were always the same: the shoe horn easing the shoe onto the right foot, the promenade in front of the mirror, the sitting down and deciding whether I liked it well enough to try on the other shoe and give it the full walk around the store. I could never say "yes" right away because then the experience would be over. So I would ask to see maybe just one more pair.

It was always difficult to decide, but usually there was one pair that made me feel special. Usually. But one time there were two pairs I could not live without. I wanted them both. Had to have them both! I begged and pleaded until my mother finally gave in. What a magnificent moment that was, walking out of Brandt's with two pairs of shoes.

Suddenly I felt an ache in my heart. On the walk over, Mom said this time we were *both* getting new shoes. Now I owned two pairs, and my mother, none. The boxes turned to lead in my hands. I said nothing for I was too horrified to speak. There was nothing that words could fix. She would have denied her need and said she would come back later, when there was more "time." I recalled the sound of my voice begging and plead-ing to "please, oh, please, please, please let me have both pairs." I wondered what had become of my awareness, just minutes earlier, of *her* need.

At birth we are totally dependent, knowing only our own needs. Survival requires we cry from those needs to get them satisfied. When survival is not the issue, we no longer need to cry; we can just ask — or whine and plead and beg: "Please Mom, please, please, please. I promise I won't ask for another thing ever if you'll just let me, give me, take me, buy me." Me, me, me.

Nothing was said about the shoes. My sadness was deep, the lesson permanent. I saw what happens when you forget about other people — kind other people, poor other people, generous other people, and any kind of other people. Sometimes you accidentally get what was meant for them . . . and sometimes it happens on purpose. In either case, you stand apart from the well-being of all and make *your* life the most important.

I hated myself and those shoes, but I never said anything. I wore them as if they were jeweled slippers, for I did not want to spoil the joy of her sacrifice.

Something happened to me as I walked out of Mr. Brandt's store. In that instant I realized: Life must be kept simple so it can be shared. One pair of shoes for everyone.

## 6 - HURT

Now I get it. This place is my past, my present, and will also be my future unless I can resolve some things. That's why this big trunk is here; it holds all the clues. This is a big, funny game for somebody. A game. Well, I won't play.

I'll just sit here, up against this dusty old trunk and wait until something happens. That's right, I'll just wait it out.

You won't catch me playing this dumb game. I don't play games anymore. You hear that, I don't play games! I'm too grown up for that stuff. So I'll just be sitting here by myself forever. And that's OK by me.

I used to play games. Or maybe I should say one particular game. It was a wonderful game for some reason. I remember it so well I can put myself right back there next to that banister on Pat Duffy's front porch. That's where the game was played. The object was to stand at the top of her stairs and then descend, saying a color on each step: "red, yellow, blue, green, gold, fire." "Fire" was the bottom step, which you'd tag with your toe and then dash back up to the top before you got caught.

It doesn't make a whole lot of sense to me now,
but I remember the feeling inside when we played.
It was the joy of friendship.

I'm sure I played all kinds of games before then. I
know I did because I had a sister who, because she
was younger than I, always agreed to any of my
games — mostly the make-believe kind which
usually consisted of pretending. Pretending we
were on a yacht (our little wooden ironing boards
turned upside down, smoking our candy cigarettes
and being very sophisticated and grown-up adults);
pretending we were cooking (the jelly beans from
our Easter Baskets or little colored macaroni
flowers from the necklaces we never made because cooking with them was more fun); pretending we were nuns (with our blanket veils and
necklace rosary beads hanging from our waists); or
priests (dispensing *Necco* wafers from a yellow cut
glass vase to rows and rows of imaginary commu-
nicants).

As I grew older, the pretending became more
serious and far more private and personal. I
imagined myself the person I wanted to be: all
grown up and on my own; attractive, unafraid,
witty. I also imagined a man who was handsome,
gentle, and brilliant, but without my incredible
sense of humor. It all fit together beautifully,
thanks to my excellent orchestration. And it kept
away the loneliness I felt.

I preferred this pretend world to the real one in which I was homely, awkward, shy, and afraid. I guess that's why the "red-yellow-blue-green-gold-fire" game made such an impression on me. The feelings of joy I experienced as part of friendship were similar to those in my pretend world.

I could have spent my whole life on that porch playing the game, but when we were in seventh grade, Pat grew up. I guess that's what you'd call it. She started going to Dayton Street with her older sister Noreen. She didn't want to be a kid anymore. She began wearing lipstick and grown-up clothes and pursuing the guys who also hung around Dayton Street.

I couldn't go with them for a lot of reasons, and it hurt to lose that part of my life. It hurt to stay behind and watch Pat grow different, grow up, grow away from anything I could participate in. I wanted what she had — something to look forward to: going to Dayton Street with Noreen at night; getting dressed up to attract someone's attention; capturing someone's glance and, finally, his desire.

Then something terrible happened. I found I could no longer escape into my dream world because I realized it was *not* a fairy tale that never comes true. It *was* coming true for Pat and probably for Noreen and for all the other girls on Dayton Street. But not for me. I felt suddenly hopeless.

I lost everything when Pat moved out of my life because I failed to realize I could share the experience of friendship with someone else. Instead I retreated into the hopelessness of my situation and waited in the background for another person with another fun game to come along and notice me. No one ever did.

Oh, other friendships came and went, but none awakened anything in me like that first one. I was always on guard, looking for signs of Dayton Street: the turning away of a glance just a hair sooner than the glance before; the return of a call just an hour past the time I felt it would be returned; the laughing becoming strained instead of exuberant. Yes, I waited for rejection, and it always came.

When the rejection didn't come from others it came from within me. It was I who didn't feel joy at hearing their voices. The thought of being with them no longer thrilled me. They became quite dull and ordinary when once they had been so special. It was I who began returning calls just a bit later than I should, turning away rather than holding a gaze, offering an obligatory chuckle or artificial smile.

I was never satisfied. Relationships could not sustain me. Not forever and sometimes hardly for a week. In this increasingly vacant and detached state, however, I discovered I could again retreat

into my fairy tale world where I was who I wanted
to be and never was hurt because life worked
there according to my script.

The more I retreated into this inner world of
mine, the less I wanted or needed to be involved
with people. Occasionally I would feel guilty about
not participating in relationships, but the lure to go
the other direction was far stronger and more
appealing. What was the harm? Maybe escaping
was part of everyone's life, and because I was so
introspective, I could create my own scenes while
others had to rely on books or movies for theirs.
This retreating could even be a very healthy thing
— filling an unmet need all on my own, without
hurting or involving anyone. Maybe I needn't
worry about it.

But I did worry, and I feared some day I would
have to give up my fantasies unless I could find a
valid reason for their growing presence.

> Come to Life.

What?

> Do not hide from hurt, from loneliness.
> Take courage. Come to life.

Where will I find this courage? I have searched and
searched and do not know where it abides. Can
you tell me, please, where I might find it?

I wait anxiously for a response, but find none.

Time passes slowly and begins to weigh heavily upon me. Sitting on the floor I lean my back against the trunk and listen for a sound — even if just the movement of air. But there is only this, the silence. Looking for direction, comfort, companionship I strain to break into that silence, searching for something within it. Like a space traveler, I wish to be transported forward into some great meaning, for there is nothing here. I quiet even my breathing and arch forward as if to invite myself in, but there is still only the thump thump thump of my heart as it keeps rhythm like a metronome, marking the passage of life.

Weary, I rest upon the floor and begin to drift off. In the distance I hear, faintly, the sing-song verses of childhood. From where are they coming? Are they "out there" or am I humming them from within? And why these chants from the past and not some magical flute beckoning me to a new, mysterious, enchanted land?

If I had different ears, could I hear something extraordinary: the commotion of life around me; the little creatures that live on my skin; atoms bumping and colliding; the energy of life; the rush of the universe? Have my ears become like filters, letting in the noises and sounds I recognize; keeping out those which have no definable tone or measurable decibel? I wonder if there are those who have learned ways of listening to sounds not heard?

What lives and moves and makes noise in the silence of infants? Is the music of life playing in the background like a pied piper, luring them forward, giving them cues? The silence of infancy is quickly shattered by the demands of caregivers: smile, turn over, open wide and say aaaah.

In adolescence, life begins to hustle from inside and out. Some hear only the call of the wild and let their bodies lead them to pleasures of the flesh, for that is the strongest and easiest-to-determine direction. Knowing only the feeling of being carried away, they allow those feelings to lead them, seeking still more pleasure. They travel even further into that blind alley until it opens into the great pit and they fall forever from grace and hope. Their lives now dependent on the needs of the flesh, their silence is engulfed in the constant and deafening screaming of those needs.

Most others travel the acceptable roads of education, marriage, family, career . . . and find not silence but the advice of all who have gone before: warning, cautioning, urging, telling, preaching, moaning, prompting, on and on through the halls of time. It is a litany whose chant is stilled only with age, because with most of life spent, foolish dreams are a waste of time. All that remains is surrender.

Bodies age, quit, decay, become what they were before it all began. But the Silence — the silence shattered at birth, the silence that worried our youth, the silence we searched out in hectic times of acquisition and accomplishment, the silence that waits like a faithful friend as we grow old and ready to listen — the Silence remains.

Can the silence from which we sprang be rediscovered before it's too late? To do so, energy, normally flowing outward in search of other energies, must be forced inward. Thoughts must be herded like stampeding cattle back into the self to halt and quiet. And when all thoughts are gone, so too will go the desire to run after them. We then stand within the void and wait patiently, calmly, empty of all we brought.

In that surrender we acknowledge life itself : before us, behind us, within us. Ebbing and flowing in the channels we forge for it . . . in the silence, the holy silence. It is before this silence that we lie prostrate on the ground of nothingness and ask of it mercy. Mercy. Not help to hang on, not favors to make it work — but mercy. Mercy in our foolishness. Mercy, for we are pitiful in our conduct and our positions of greed and power. Mercy, because we have been so lost and confused.

The silence must be this and only this: complete absence of me and my feeble hopes and attempts to hang on to the "things" in life. It is only when my poverty runs so deep it takes with it all I have and am that I can approach the threshold of the Silent and beg entry, admission. For the silence is nothing and yet all.

Yes, I am alone at last. The noises, the songs, the words, the thoughts have been stilled. The Silence has come now and surrounds me. This is the great moment, the moment of surrender.

Frantic, I jump to my feet and cry out in terror. Help! Is there anyone out there who can help me?

And the sound of my voice shatters the silence.

The door looms before me, casting its angry
shadow across the floor. Please forgive me. I am
afraid and do not understand what is required of
me.

Weak with discouragement I lie down. The
shadow falls upon me. No! I must continue or be
lost forever to the search.

I rise and try to move the trunk to the door,
hoping if I stand on top of it I will be tall enough to
search for a key, perhaps hidden atop the frame.
But the trunk will not budge. It is too heavy, and
wears me out trying to push and shove it. Its
weight and contents come, no doubt, from my
many years of collecting.

I sit back to rest and am suddenly reminded of
Uncle Frank. At the house following his burial I
looked at all his knickknacks, miscellaneous items,
and memorabilia from different places. A second
before his death these were his treasures. Now
they were rubble, in the way of the next inhabitant
of that space.

Frank, you have left behind your precious things,
and those things only make us sad because nobody
loves them the way you did. It would have been
better when you left to have all your things put in

the ground with you, for they have no meaning to anyone here. And they also have no meaning to you now. So what were they for?

What were they for? I open my trunk and look over its contents. There are countless "necessities": homes with their mortgages (and insurance policies); a few automobiles (and *their* insurance policies); the rugs, drapes and furnishings for probably 30 or 40 rooms; china, silverware and crystal service for twelve; magazine subscriptions by the score; albums and envelopes of photos capturing significant and not so significant moments; the clothes of several generations and fads; hundreds of shoes, some almost unworn; enough cookbooks to stock a library; appliances to facilitate anything you might do in the kitchen; chic little items like napkin rings (a real necessity); pens with my name on them which still ended up in someone else's room; jewelry for every occasion; equipment for several hobbies and crafts; a 25 cubic foot freezer unplugged and stuffed to the brim with, of all things, yarn (what a terrific sale that was); and a file cabinet to hold all the articles I clipped on being less materialistic.

What had I been thinking? In such a short while I have accumulated so much "stuff" I can no longer even manage it. Why do we accumulate so many things? They bring us pleasure, I suppose, at least for a while. Their acquisition, perhaps, gives us a feeling of accomplishment. When we are small, we must beg and plead to get our little hearts' desires. As we get older, we find we have the power to get whatever we want and we want it all.

Sitting here now, however, I see my pursuit of "happiness" has made this trunk so heavy I can't even move it. I must discard some of its contents, but what can I bear to part with? Certainly the brass spitoon, and maybe the yarn. Probably the sterling silver gravy boat (doesn't look like I'll be having any company). Not the home. I need the home. But if I keep the home, I will need all that goes with it: the insurance, the furniture, the tools, the appliances, the cookbooks, and my job with its requirements (wardrobe, car, computers) so I can afford to keep the home. Could I live without a home? Where would I stay? In someone else's home? That doesn't seem fair. In my car? Whoops! On the streets?

Maybe there would be nothing wrong with living on the streets. It would certainly put me in touch with something very basic — my dependence on all that is around me. I'd be forced to look at people and life differently.

The homeless would surely think me a fool to envy their hardships. Maybe I am wrong about how rich that life could be, but I'm not wrong about all this "stuff." The acquisition and upkeep of these foolish treasures have robbed me of most of my time and hold me back from taking the next step. I am ready now to get rid of my things.

I stand before this trunk which holds the life I thought was important, and begin discarding its contents. As I work my way to the bottom I can see something is written under the very last item. I almost topple inside in my eagerness to get to the message: "This trunk is for holding those things you value. If one thing remains so does the trunk. If the trunk is empty it is no longer a trunk."

And it vanished, leaving me free to travel unencumbered to the next place.

## 9 - BEAUTY

I feel stunned for a moment, almost in shock. I
have nothing to worry about. Nothing!

Then anxiety creeps back in. It starts with "what
will happen if " and has no single-thought ending
because they all flood back — the fears, the wor-
ries, the doubts.

I force them away. There is no need for anything
in this place, I can see that. But what about the
next place? No, there is no need for anything
there either. But suppose there is no next place?
Suppose that door opens into nothing and even I
disappear? I've just given away all I worked so hard
for on the chance there is something better. I
could probably get all my things back with a wish,
but somehow they are no longer important. I must
try to reason forward.

I am trusting my experience, following something
within. While I am stunned, I also feel excited
about discoveries that lie ahead. Ahead. I must
not look back.

Fear no longer has a place in my life, for I came
here eager to learn and have nothing now to lose.
Fear listens to shouts from the crowd warning of
dangers lying in wait should one stray from the

norms *they* have lived by. "Believe as we believe or something terrible will happen . . . to all of us. Stay here where it is safe — do not go into the cave where, we have been warned, lives a dragon. If you go you may bring danger to all our lives. Stay, you must stay."

I can't stay. I can't. Don't you see? Something wonderful has happened to me and I can remain here no longer. I must be on my way.

I am running now, far away from the crowd. I can still hear their anxious sounds, see their fists raised in anger. Some have broken away and are coming after me. They may catch up, but I will not go back. I am free, exhilarated. I run and run and run. Suddenly, I am in a field of light. Exhausted from the run, I drop to the ground.

This feels like a new place. I have found the still point between being and belief. Here I am but a springing forth. Like the flowers and green things, I too have my season, my particular beauty. I will follow the scent of the jasmine, the song of the bird and see where they lead.

I am so happy here. There is only beauty now. It is all around me. I can feel it. And I am a part of this beauty. I will never go back.

The worried voices of the crowd are gone. It is easier now to still my mind and be patient — to wait in terrifying anticipation of the great moment — for I believe I have stumbled upon the threshold of God.  There will be a visit soon.

# 10 - THE PRESENCE

It is quiet now as I await my visitor. A terrifying beauty. That is how it will come to me. Will there be wings? Radiance? A face? Light? Glowing? Music? Will it be at all familiar? I wait.

There is nothing.

Must I sit here empty or can I go outward to greet my guest? Are there things I could do to hasten the visit? A chant, perhaps, a meditation? Is it better to have no thoughts of my own, or is there one particular word that will bring it down upon me? I am a stranger to this land. I will do nothing but hold to the stillness. And wait.

I am standing on the ground of my being. I have only the life within me. All else has fallen away. The fragrance around me is like an opiate, and I drift into the comfort of my bedroom back home.

I used to hate sleep because it took away so many precious hours from my schedule. But lately I find it deep and mysterious, freeing me to journey into the dark sky where the moon in full splendor beckons me. Shall I go just one time?

My bed shakes and I am frozen with fear. "Gumba, Gumba!" I call out the cat's name, hoping to feel his paws pounce upon me in playfull recognition. I lift my head and turn toward the direction of the movement. The cat is not there. Nothing is there.

I tense and prepare to bolt from my bed. What if "it" comes after me? Can I outrun its reach, its touch? My eyes search the darkness again for the cat. I call his name: "Come on Gumba, come on." He is not here. I am alone with this presence.

My body is rigid and I cannot move. I exist on two planes. I know everything in this darkness because I put it there: the furnishings, pictures, clock, the heap of crumpled clothes, the dress hanging on the closet door. There are no mysteries in this room by day. But this night, this night has brought me something I do not know and I am terrified.

Why am I so afraid of this particular darkness? It is different; I am different.

Once before, I glimpsed something beyond — something wonderful. I could not stand in the same spot to know it. Tears poured forth and I began running through the house crying and shouting "yes, yes, yes." Then it left, as suddenly and mysteriously as it came. Strangely though, my life did not change because of that moment. I went back to peeling potatoes at the sink. The sink in the house on Walton Street, in the neighborhood of Austin, the city of Chicago, the state of Illinois, country of the United States, continent of North America, on the planet earth, in the fiery hot, icy cold, airless, weightless, mysterious, frightening, and never-ending regions of space — the domain of God.

From early childhood it was all the unanswered questions that bothered me. Some of those questions were not supposed to be asked, I guess, out of respect. I couldn't comply. I kept asking and found answers.

Other questions could have no answers, but did that mean they could not be felt or voiced? My life became a deliberate search for answers and it was the persistence of my questions that created a path, a space that attracted the bolt of lightning which answered them all in a flash: the ones you could know and the ones beyond knowing.

From that confoundedly unspeakable domain of God — without voice, without word — came a knowing more than I could fit in this little brain, a feeling more than I could experience in this little heart, an answer so vast I could not stand in one spot to gather it all. I had to run wildly from room to room to make myself big enough, to keep myself in one piece. My desire to know, my determination to search, had created an emptiness, a void, a place for truth.

That truth still a memory within me, I call out to my visitor. "I know you are near, I can feel your touch on my bed. Snatch me from the shape of my darkness, lift me from this realm of shadows that tease and terrify me. I am ready. I stand guard over nothing, have nothing to take with. I am ready. Yes, I am ready."

The scream was horrifying as it tore through the silence and woke me. The voice was my own, still bouncing off of walls somewhere in time and space.

I open my eyes and am again in the waiting place.

I stand and stretch. From my hand falls a piece of
soft gray and white fur. I pick it up and rub it
gently across my cheek. Gumba, I can almost feel
your heart beating within this little tuft.

Oh, what a fine creature you are, my friend. What
a magnificently fine creature. Your eyes look to
me with such trust and warmth. I cannot believe
there is no intent in that heart of yours. You are
part of the dream — the dream I hold deep within.

The trees, the waters, the sun, the creatures that
fly, swim, scamper, and walk — we are all filled
with creation. In the bird's ascent and graceful
motion I can recognize the hand. In the powerful
movements of the waters ending with a splash on
the shore I feel the source. With the bright green
shoots of new life coming from branches so brittle
they would snap the day before, I recognize the
timing of it all. Today, today and not a moment
sooner. Today, today and not a moment later.
Today, today is the exact right time.

Today, let it spring forth. Today, let it take you
over. Begin the run, spread your wings, run, run,
run until you can lift your feet and soar into the air.
Let the waters within you, beneath you, heave and
commence their unceasing roll toward a somewhere distant shore. Today, hear your heart beat

in rhythm with the universe. Then try to hold it
back. Just try. Desire will overcome you and you
will be unable to resist, unable to contain it. You
will feel the rumble of life itself, for you will be
standing on the ground of your being, the ground of
*all* being.

From that day forward you will be unrecognizable
even to yourself. You will respond in total obedience to the movement of life within you, just like
the birds and the flowers and the oceans. That
which transforms energy into matter — makes you
move and breathe and live — will become undeni-
able.

This awareness is what fills me now — touching and
terrifying me. What a fool I am to wish it be
something I can define and dismiss.

The heresy trial was quick and to the point:
". . . and the third item on the agenda will be the
meetings being held in the Garrisons' home." My
shock at hearing this blurted out with no warning
— not even a lessening of the smiles that greeted
us one minute before — blew item one and two
right off the agenda. I came to the meeting with a
concern for the non-keeping of Lent in our parish.
But good old item three changed the direction of
those energies within me and became a turning
point in my life.

There are no real villains in this story. My life was made up of lots of people — most of them well-meaning, some of them well-educated, many of them sweet-and-sour harmless sorts of people who all believed in something. They seldom questioned, or if they did, they put the answers in a place marked "for later" and went along with the group. Perhaps they never accepted their own experience as worthy — denying their own life's passion and significance in favor of membership.

I remember sitting, at age 10, in the darkened church on Good Friday with the family Bible on my lap. The print was so small, the church so dark, it made reading almost impossible. I was drawn to the experience. Something called me to the darkness, the quiet, the flickering candlelight, the stillness, the smell of incense, the thought of death. It all set the scene for something almost primitive . . . like the caves from which young boys emerged men.

I could not resist the call to experience life and death and great courage. I wanted to hang from that cross and see if I could stand the pain; to walk the path and see if believing in something made me unafraid of the outcome; to go right through the moment of final breath and see what it feels like to be dead. I wanted to have that whole intense and horrifying experience; to know what it's like to be filled with unswerving conviction from within.

I followed the call. Like Adam and Eve, I was driven by the desire to know more. I became the initiator of my own life, gave birth to myself, fell from paradise.

It was perfection sitting around the table at that parish council meeting. Centuries of infallible perfection. In spite of the warnings, I had tasted the forbidden fruit from the tree of life and the voice came thundering down upon me: "If what I hear you are saying is true, then I am concerned it is heresy. You are very visible in the parish and I don't want anyone to think you are speaking for the Church."

I was not banished from the garden. Rather than defend or deny my own experience, I left willingly.

Fear and sadness overcame me. For the first time in my life I was standing alone; not part of a community of faith. I was afraid God would not find me, for surely I, on my own, had no power or ability to make the ritualistic connection. But I would not be alone for long. Someone will call.

Someone who was a repeated and treasured guest in my home will call. Someone who greeted me as friend and accepted my kindness will call. Someone who blessed me for my works of mercy will call. Someone, surely, will call.

Gumba pressed against me and the warmth from
his body took the chill from my heart. A tear
trickled slowly down my cheek and dropped into
his soft gray fur. He purred as if he, himself, felt
the pain.

All I believed in died during those next few disap-
pointing weeks. That is why I went in search of a
better place, a place I knew existed because I had
glimpsed it in moments that became part of me.
And I found it — just as I remembered. Found it
here in this place whose door opens in. Only
beauty surrounds me now, and I am a part of this
beauty. I will never go back. Never.

But wait. The others! They do not know of this
place. They are afraid of the dark and won't go
into the cave they have been warned about. I
must go back and tell them, for they have buried
deep within their hearts a lie, a lie that is called
insignificance.

Thinking they are small and worthless, they hold
on to each other's hands and tremble at the
thought of greatness, as if they deserve no part.
Believing in nothing, they make tabernacles of their
lives and within them hold sacred those things that
are of no consequence. They are afraid to let go
of their precious things, their impressive titles,
their signs of worth, even their poverty and strife
— for it is all they have, and, they fear, all there is.

Please, Gatekeeper, I beg leave now for I must go back and tell the others of this place. They have been my companions for so long I cannot bear the thought of leaving them behind. Life here belongs also to them, and they do not know it.

Let me go back. I shall leave my heart in this place so you know I must return. If I am not back in a day, my heart is yours to give to someone else.

# INTERMISSION

Stop! Stop! Stop! This is all getting just too confusing. I can't figure out what is going on here.
First she's in this place with a door that's not a
door, then she's in some enchanted land waiting
for God to appear, and now she's leaving her heart
and going back for a day. To where . . . and from
where? What is it all supposed to mean?

Yes, it is confusing, but don't you get it? There is
this one question around which we write, com-
pose, paint, sculpt, ponder, and try to live: What is
life — all life, this life? Is death the end or will
there be something more? The answers lie in a
place we cannot touch from here . . . although
artists try.

Now do you sort of understand what is going on?
I am trying to take you with me to the tormented
place I have always gone alone. It may feel like a
form of madness, but isn't it absolutely exquisite?

Of late there is this feeling, almost like a spell, that
has come over me, calling me down to my basement in the wee hours of the morning to write.
But I am not writing a book as everyone thinks. I
am recording something quite astonishing that is
being told to me. Why me? Because I ask questions, then wait for answers . . . knowing they do
come.

Many things come to me as a total surprise, and I find myself in tears. These moments are so exciting that I don't want to leave "the waiting place" and go to my nine-to-five job.

If I've been obedient to the message, and not gotten *my* words in the way, you will feel something quite profound in it all. So stay with me if you can. I am as baffled as you how this will end. I do, however, hold out the possibility that I will not write the conclusion, at least not from this side. I have documented all my work and leave with it the instruction: "If I am unable, print out the titles listed on this disk. They are worthy work."

So, please return with me to my waiting place, for I have put myself in great danger to speak with you. There is but a minute left on the clock, and I can hear in the distance the sound of the Gatekeeper's keys.

Quickly, quickly, my hand. Take my hand.

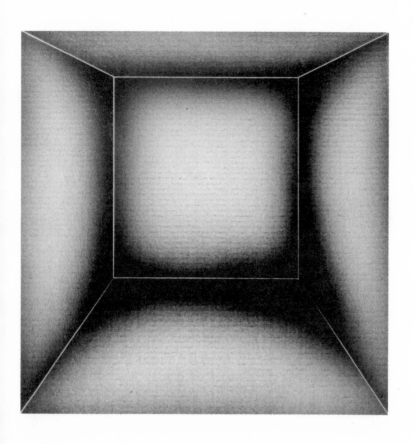

I'm getting used to the way this place feels. Sort of liking it. Maybe I'll remain here forever — retreat deeper and deeper into myself until I am totally removed from life as I have known it. Or maybe I'll have some sort of explosive thought and be catapulted back to where I was, only transformed somehow. How will it all end? Or begin? Or continue? Where am I?

> This is the place where Truth resides.

Yes, indeed. I'm beginning to know what that means.

> Bring them back.

Bring who back?

> All of them.

If you mean the people in my life, I won't! I see no point to that. Why bring anyone back? They are a part of my life that is over, done. I have learned my lessons and am trying to think differently, believe differently, live differently. Isn't that enough?

> Why have you come to this place?

I don't know.  It seems like I woke up one day and I was here.

You must have followed some definite path.

Yes, it certainly felt that way.

And where did you want the path to lead?

To goodness, holiness.

Are you holy yet?

No, not yet.

What are you?

I'm alone.

Do you want to stay alone?

Yes.

Then why do you pound on that door;
why do you want to leave?

Good question.  I don't know.  Something inside makes me do it.  I guess I want to feel something.  Not the usual things.  I want to feel something quite extraordinary.

Do you think you are ready?

I have traveled round and round in search of this place, come here with great hope, risking all I have and am. I am finally on the threshold. It is time for my next lesson. Yes, it is time. I am ready to experience truth.

The people you injured, the wrong things you set in motion, the missed opportunities?

I am very sad about all that. I tried to fix some of it.

But you can't, can you? Life — theirs, yours, all life — was directly affected by your participation in it. You had it within your power to build up or tear down, to enable or cripple, to create or destroy.

What is the point of this conversation?

What is the point of anything?

I don't know anymore. To learn something? To teach something? To share something? Maybe to be a sign . . . a multi-dimensional, flashing, beeping, whirling sign in the road so no one will lose the way.

Some of the people in your life may have lost their way because of you. Go get them. Bring them back.

Bring them back? Who? Which ones? Some are already gone. For some it is, probably, no longer possible. Others seem happy, why take the chance of hurting them? You are asking an impossible task of me — a task I don't understand. With age I have grown cautious, wary of my motives because I am weak with fault, and fear doing even more damage because of a need to cleanse myself. I would rather suffer the loss of my own life than to commit one more selfish act.

> *That* is the holiness you seek. With this feeling in your heart, do not be afraid to greet all who come. It will set your final example — how you shall be known.

Yes, yes, I want everyone to know what I learned and loved and will miss so dearly. But just *thinking* of leaving is sad. And what will I say? Certainly not goodbye, for there is more. Nor do I know where to tell them to look for me.

> When you have spoken, they will know where to find you.

Please, I can't. This hurts too much.

> Speak.

"Bring them back?" "Speak?" This is becoming too ordinary to lead to anything transcendent. I am looking for something outside this realm: angels, visions, haze in the distance — something I can't quite make out and therefore must judge to be from a higher plane. Something spectacular. Something that is probably right on the other side of that door. Maybe I'll just open it a crack and see what is there.

The knob turns easily now, the door opens outward. My heart begins to pound in anticipation of what I am about to encounter. Before I can determine who or what is out there, my daughter appears before me.

Kimberly, what are you doing here?

> You tell me, Mother; you're the answer
> lady. You always seem to know everything.
> I still hear your voice, know what you
> would say in every instance. You did a
> good job on me, Mother!

Are you being snotty?

> I don't think so, but then again I really don't
> know. I almost never know what you are

talking about. Why don't we bring in Vicki, she would probably know. In fact, let's bring in the whole gang so you can hear what we all have to say.

Do I want to hear what you have to say?

I understand you are here searching out truth.

And *you* have it?

Now who's being snotty! Yes, I have my truth; are you interested in it?

I don't know. It could be painful.

You always said that is how we grow. Not to run away from pain. Remember when Laurie Hellinka was kicking me in the knees all day long under my desk and I came home crying? You told me about how cruel people can be and how harmful it would be for you to get involved, that I would never get strong and learn how to work with life if you went to school and handled it for me. Remember?

Yes. I even remember standing on the third step down in the basement with you on the landing so we were almost eye to eye. The anguish I felt at that moment was perhaps as great as your dread of the next day with Laurie. Was I really helping you or was I just not wanting to get involved in a messy situation? Did I sacrifice you to my own coward-ice? At the time I had both feelings running side by side within me. Which was the actual motivation: the good, nurturing one . . . or the selfish one?

> So that's what you're doing here, asking yourself whether you were a good mother. Or are you asking me?

I know better than to ask either one of us that question, because neither answer really matters. I was what I was.

> Sounds good to me! Now can I leave?

I guess so.

> I'll send Vicki in.

Hey, wait, maybe I don't want to be doing this.

> Hi, Maman.

Hi, Vic. How are you?

> Well, I'm pretty good actually. Last week was bad but this next one should be better.

Oh, really?  What happened last week?

> It's the end of the school year and my
> students feel like they can just drift off
> instead of paying attention.  I teach up to
> the last second of the year, so a lot of my
> time is spent trying to discipline them.

Ah, yes, discipline.  That was always my battle cry:
discipline.  Although with you, Vic, it was almost
automatic.  You seemed to take charge of your life
from the beginning.  Was that because you saw me
so involved in my own life you sort of knew you
were on your own?

> I don't know.  I didn't see you that way.  At
> least I don't think I did.  Are you OK,
> Maman?

Yes.

> Well, if you don't need me I guess I'll be
> leaving.

Don't need you?

> Well, yes.  I don't see any of your usual pots
> and pans or heaps of yarn scattered about,
> so I'm assuming you're here to do some
> heavy-duty thinking, and for that you always
> needed your quiet time.

Hmmmm, yes, quiet time. Well, I'm glad you
dropped by.

You bet. Take care, Maman.

Bye, Vic.

Does Mom want to see me next?

Deb? Is that you out there?

Hey, Mamma Doo.

Deb, what's going on?

Nothing really. I just saw Vic leave and
heard your voice in here.

Isn't this strange? It feels like I'm saying goodbye.

Don't talk like that; you're gonna make me
sad.

This is getting to be like one of those sappy movies
where the dying mother calls all her children close
to her and says her final words.

You're not dying are you?

We're all in the process of dying, aren't we?

No. I mean *really* dying.

I don't think so.

What did you say to Kim and Vic?

Not much. They stopped by and we chatted for a minute or two. But I didn't say much of anything.

Well, don't say anything to me either, OK?

OK.

Do you want any water? A blanket or something?

No. Thanks anyway.

Why don't you leave? This place is kind of lonely.

I'm not through doing something very important . . . I think.

Will you be OK?

Yes, Deborah. I don't want you to worry about me.

I guess I'll be goin' then.

OK. Bye, Deb.

Jimmy, you're next.

This is stupid. I'm not going in there!

Jimmy, you better go in. Mom wants to see you.

OK, OK, don't push me. Hey, Dude, Deb said you wanted to see me.

Jimmy, I did not ask to see you.

OK. Bye.

Wait a minute. Don't go yet. So, what's going on?

Nothing.

Jimmy, are you sure?

Yep. Hey, man, this place gives me the creeps.

I know.

Why don't you just leave?

I can't.

Oh, yeah.  You haven't analyzed everything yet.

That's real nice, Jim.

I see you're here alone.  Where are all the down-and-outers you usually hang out with?

I needed to be alone.

I get the message.  See ya later.

Wait. Jim?  Oh well!

That was short and to the point.  I guess they didn't want to hang around too long for fear of getting another one of my famous lectures; or worse than that, winding up in one of my charac-ter-building exercises like "The Parable of the Onion Rings."  I bet they never forgot that one.

I felt money was not to be wasted on things that weren't necessities.  And it was I who determined what necessity meant.  Going out to eat was not one of them.  On the other hand, there were all these fast food places tempting customers to drive on in. Jack-in-the-Box restaurants were the great-est lure for us.

After a particularly testy week at home, I agreed to a luncheon outing.  Ordering was always a major problem — the kids wanted it all and felt hungry enough to consume it. But I knew only a relatively small portion would be eaten before the "I'm too full, do I have to finish this?" chant would begin. Hating to waste food or money, I decided it was a good opportunity to teach my children about harmony and trust.

Everyone wanted onion rings. "Yes!" And a whole order at that. "Yes, I can too eat them all!"

The instructions went like this: I will get only two orders of onion rings for the four of you. You will pretend there are tons of onion rings here and you can eat as much as you want. You must not look at the others' places to see how fast they are eating or how much they have piled before them. When you want another onion ring because you really have a taste for it, you may take another one from the bag. You must not check the bag to see how many are left. Ask only of yourself: Am I enjoying this? If you reach for another onion ring and the bag is empty, I will buy another bag and will con- tinue to do so until everyone has had enough. This is the test: Can you live with only your honest need, or will your fears and greed create an appe- tite for more than it takes to be satisfied?

"Four hamburgers and two orders of onion rings please." I then sat back and watched the lesson unfold.

It didn't work. Eyes were darting every which way. Hands, still greasy from the last grab, grabbed again and again. While no one actually complained to me, there was the usual cloaked form of tattling: "Jimmy, did you hear what Mom said? Only take another one when you *really* want it."

I did not have to buy another bag to satisfy anyone's need because, before the meal was over, they all developed stomach aches from the tension. No one actually tasted what was eaten. Nothing was learned. What was reinforced, however, was that they never knew what Mom was going to do next, but for sure it would spoil a good time.

Maybe that's why they left here in such a hurry. I know, I'll leave them a note in case they ever return.

Dearest Children,

I don't know if I could have loved you then as much as I do now. We spent so many difficult years together in the struggle to grow. I was a child when I had you. I knew what was wrong in me and tried to fix it in you — to make you strong so your life would serve others instead of always being stuck to itself out of fear.

Some of my weaknesses brought pain to your small and innocent lives. Life should have been spread out before you like a grand adventure. Instead I shoved you face first into cold, hard reality. "Who said life is fair?" I asked over and over as I prepared you for that "unfair" life. I tried to make you strong so you would not feel the pain of disappointment; would not bring that pain back to me where I was hiding.

In spite of my shortcomings, there was something solid and strong deep within me. I could feel it. I believed this inner strength was very important, so I structured your early life like mine was, to encourage the journey inward.

To accomplish this I gave you very little of what
the world offered. We lived in a neighborhood
where friendship was not that readily available, so
you were forced to spend most of your time
alone. I felt being your own person was far more
valuable than being like everyone else, so I kept
your life simple, bare, different from most of the
other children who were your peers.

I stayed home until the last of you went to school.
While I was always there, I don't remember ever
spending time with any one of you reading or
playing games or getting involved with the routines
of your little lives. Instead, I kept a constant eye
on your feelings, making sure you never suffered
alone. I taught you how to think and reason and
interpret those feelings. Even as children you
spoke with wisdom and insight. You became my
teachers and my inspiration.

Then it happened, a horrifying moment for all of
us. I packed a bag and left our home. Lacking real
courage, I ran away without you. The pain of that
moment must be with you still. All I had ever told
you about being strong, about facing problems,
about loving you, must have become lies. All the
wonderful times we shared as part of a bustling
family must have dimmed in the flash of that
moment. I returned for you, but foundations had
been shaken.

Some acts I committed were wrong but innocent:
marrying too young, too needy; bringing children
into the world when I was not ready to sacrifice;
hiding my real needs because I was not brave
enough to insist they be met. The final act, however — choosing my pain over yours — was and is
unforgivable. Therefore, it is not forgiveness I
seek, but understanding and compassion.

In our brokenness we are sometimes unable or
unwilling to rise out of our own desperate needs
and care about others. A life well-lived, however,
grows steadily toward love for others, and is one
day blessed with the grace to forgive itself and
move on. This I have done.

If I could live it all over? I would do exactly as I
have done, because I was following something that
taught me — sometimes gently, sometimes se-
verely — what it means to be human. I tried to
direct you toward that something I felt and heard;
something I still hear — the Voice. It speaks the
same message I heard when I was a child sitting in
that dark church on Good Friday; it speaks the
same message I heard in Jack-in-the-Box; it speaks
the same message I hear now.

My dearest children, I will cherish forever the brief
but everlasting time we had together. We shared
the same body until life called you forth. While
you are all grown up now and gone from my days
— never will you be gone from my heart.

## 15 - HATE

Grandpa!  I knew you'd show up sooner or later.
You must have heard my story of the onion rings
and figured out I was trying to teach something you
did not learn.

> You are being very hard on me.

You deserve it.

> So now what do I say?

What do you want to say?

> I want to tell you to mind your own busi-
> ness.

I am.

> It doesn't sound like it to me.  It sounds like
> you're minding mine.

There was a lot to mind.

> How do you know?

I was there, remember?

> No, I don't remember this angry woman.

I wasn't angry then. Well, maybe I was. But I had a right.

> Tell me, what right was that?

The right to live a good life.

> And how did I deny you that right?

You were selfish and greedy.

> That may be true, but didn't you still have a good life?

Yes, I guess so.

> So then what right are we talking about?

I had the right to love or to hate you.

> And you chose hate.

Yes.

> Yet you are still not satisfied with hating me. You want something more.

I want to be able to hate you even harder.

> What would that accomplish?

If my hate was stronger, I could probably get other people to hate you too.

Without even knowing me?

I would tell them about you, and then they would know you.

Then by all means, tell them about me.

I already did.

Do they hate me?

I suspect they feel my anger but can't hate you because you're not around. Maybe they will take that anger and use it to hate someone in their own life.

So it's spreading.

I guess so. Probably yes.

Is that what you want to do with your life, spread hate over the earth?

I'm not spreading hate. People are bringing hate upon themselves by being selfish and self-centered. It's not wrong to hate something evil.

I heard you talking about choices. Do you have a choice in this?

Yes. And I am choosing to hate you.

Does the Voice encourage you in this?

The Voice says nothing about that.

I hear the Voice.

Did the Voice encourage you to take two pork chops?

The Voice said nothing about that.

Grandpa, I don't want to talk anymore. Please go away. Maybe later on I will be able to discuss this, but right now I can't give in so easily. I have lived my whole life motivated by anger of one kind or another. I don't know how to live without it. Please go away, Grandpa. Please, just go away.

I have lived my whole life motivated by anger. The
anger seemed to counteract the fear that was ever
present and made me determined, strong. It felt
like passion, fervor; it gave me direction. Without
anger I lacked courage.

I've often wondered what put the anger there —
the anger that was part of my mother's whole
family. Their stories started sweetly and ended
with red faces and pounding fists. "If she thinks for
a minute that she is going to . . . she is badly mis-
taken!" "So I thought to myself, just go ahead and
try it. You'll be sorry!" Mom used to say about
Grandpa that he would get a look in his eye "like
the devil himself."

Around others we were generally a calm and
pleasant group, even cheerful and happy-go-lucky.
When left to ourselves, however, we would begin
to think, and those second thoughts suddenly took
on suspicious, unfriendly tones. Our memories
wound up totally opposite of the original experience — almost as if there were something within us
transposing what actually happened. People were
out to "get us" or take advantage of us; and you
could expect nothing but the absolute worst from
someone, that was for sure.

The oldest two, my mother and aunt, tell stories of how they had their dreams shattered by their mother's demands of them. The family had to be supported and, being the oldest, they were expected to do it.

Getting married and leaving the house was also a bit touchy. Losing those paychecks would have been disastrous, so Grandma did all she could to discourage and postpone the marriages. When they were finally unavoidable, she greeted them with comments designed to insure that guilt accompany any future happiness.

Grandma, I just don't know about you. You looked so sweet, but your children's stories are so bitter and vicious that I don't know what to believe. The poison in their systems . . . how did it get there? Was it in their blood from the start because their father was a man with "the devil in his eyes"? Were they transfused with something that came from deep within you, like envy? Or did blind obedience to the wrong things break their spirit — breed pessimism and deep resentment?

It was so difficult for me to comprehend the messages I got from Mom about my uncles and aunts. They will "kill me" when they find out I broke the glass on the coffee table or lost one of the earrings that was part of my halloween costume or burned spaghetti onto the bottom of

Grandma's favorite pot. They will *kill* me. But
they never did. They usually reacted with warmth
and concern. These people loved me, and I knew
it. Why was I being told my world was filled with
cruel and harsh people? Was my mother's world
filled with this sort of violence?

I think perhaps it was, because to take away one's
dream is certainly to bring death to the heart of a
person. Mom lost everything she wanted to life's
circumstances until she finally determined that this
was what life is: giving up, losing, regretting, resent-
ing. She experienced disappointment after disappointment, blindly obeying until all that remained
was resignation. Her way of living was too passive
and sad for me to adopt, so I anxiously awaited the
time I would have life in my own hands.

As I grew older, I discovered several methods of
handling my needs. I could learn to live with them;
ask; manipulate someone; or just take!

Most of my childhood I chose to live with my
needs  because asking, manipulating or taking
brought too much guilt and concern for my poor
widowed mother. Grandma was constantly re-
minding me how hard my mother's life was and
making sure I didn't take advantage of her (the way
she did, I suspect). According to Grandma,
everything I did was burdensome and hurtful for
Mom: wanting to go out with my friends on her

birthday (New Year's Eve), having a friend over, doing things that would make her worry (which was anything that took me out of her sight). There would be no bicycle (I think because a bicycle meant going farther than the three squares of sidewalk that could be seen from the upstairs window). Yes, it seemed everything I wanted was a problem.

My mother was not being cruel, just afraid. Not wanting to be hurt and disappointed one more time, she just resigned herself and hung on tight to what she had.

The anger? No wonder! There was something magnificent inside my family trying to get out and search and find and become. But walls were put up, and written on them, in big bold letters, was the death sentence: "Honor thy Father and thy Mother!"

I am here, in this place, because I escaped that sentence.

My father's blood delivered me here. I am told of his great love. He was a wonderful person — generous, fun-loving, gentle yet strong. He genuinely liked people and they could feel it. There were no "second thoughts" creeping in to spoil everything. Coming from a large and outgoing Italian family, Dad found himself right at home with all my mother's brothers and sisters — calling them "the kids" and treating them as if they were his own.

I'm not sure what attracted him to my mother; she certainly could not have been too dynamic or outgoing. Her time was spent listening to the radio and reading Street & Smith romance magazines. It was a broken radio that forced her to call my dad, the radio repairman down the street, to "please come look at it."

I imagine her shy, resigned to having nothing but her fantasies — preferring reading about life to actually participating in it. His family lived in another city, so maybe that is what drew him to her. She was part of a large family all living together in a small apartment. He enjoyed people and here were all the people you could possibly want under one roof. Since he had the only car in the family, he would pack everyone he could into it for weekend outings. I think my mother was important, but only part of the whole package.

Great Grandma called him, in German, "that dirty Italian." And Grandma was, of course, resentful of his presence in her family's life. Oh, she accepted the favors all right, but she did not want any love or gratitude going outward from her family toward him. These were feelings that belonged exclusively to her and Grandpa. Besides, Dad was not to be trusted, for surely he was being kind for some reason that would benefit him rather than us.

Grandma convinced my mother the family could not survive without her, so she and Dad were engaged five years before my father decided that was long enough. Grandma and Great Grandma sputtered and fussed, but the marriage eventually took place.

Dad brought joy into our lives and was loved by everyone who knew him. His sudden death was a tragedy for the entire family. He left behind a widow in her seventh month of pregnancy and a four-year old daughter who became, from that moment forward, Sorrow.

How would Sorrow live without Joy? Soon there was born into Sorrow's darkness Hope. Hope, in the form of a beautiful new life, a sister. Now there would be two of us who had blood that was richer because of our father's love. She was another good seed planted in the angry and suspicious soil of mother's family.

# 18 - STRENGTH

Thinking back, I remember how every now and then my grandmother would suggest I was involved in something totally out of place for somebody like me. Surprised by her accusations, I would want to laugh but couldn't because I'd be dumbfounded how this puritan woman ever conceived of such an idea. A church-going woman with God on her lips and a rosary in her hand, thinking things like that? Grandma, I have such confused feelings about you. Could you come, sit here by me so we can talk?

Grandma, you gave me so many good things. You were one of the most determined and strong women I know. You raised eight children and helped in the raising of many of your grandchildren. We all speak of you with such fondness, each having a wonderful memory of the things you showed or taught or gave us. Yet you died all alone on the floor of a nursing home. Why do you think that is?

> I don't know. Eight children and none of them had room for me in their home?

Some of your daughters even took in their husband's mothers and cared for them. Doesn't that surprise you?

They probably did it for the same reasons I did the things I did, to please their husbands.

Why was that so important to you?

Women need their men.

Women need men, but only when they are good persons. No woman needs a man who is damaged. He will only introduce that damage into the lives of those around him. I guess you never realized that.

I was what I was. Isn't that what I heard you tell your kids a little while ago?

Yes, and my mother was what she was. But I am trying to become more than who I am. I am trying to become who I can be.

What is that supposed to mean?

There is an energy in life that seeks a higher purpose than self. When you try to harness that energy and direct it where it does not belong, you destroy the joy of life and bring about anger, resentment, depression, sadness. When we wanted to love others we were told we had to love Grandpa first. When we wanted to serve others we were told we must serve Mother first. When we wanted to learn and grow we were held down by chains of loyalty and guilt. It was all wrong.

It is good that you have learned all this in
spite of me, honey.

Are *you* being snotty now Grandma?

I am dead and gone from your life, and still
you fight me?

No one is ever dead and gone.  Your deeds live on
in those who were in any way a part of your life.  It
has taken me a long time, but I am finally coming to
grips with some things that have bothered me.
Hurt can take place even in the most loving of
relationships.

What matters is that you live what you
truly believe.  That is what you will take to
your final moment.

Your final moment was on the floor of a nursing
home on your way back from the bathroom.

I know.  They said I should call for help
when I was done.

And did you?  Did you call for help and no one
came, or did they not come fast enough for you?
Or were you just sick and tired of being dependent
on people and decided to take your life into your
own hands?

Why do you want to know this?

I want to know what you felt in that last moment.

So you won't feel guilty?

So I won't feel sad.

Why would you feel sad? You talk about
life being a journey each person must make
alone.

But, Grandma, you had eight children. As much as
some of them resented your hold on their life,
they all talk about your constant care: their little
white shoes you scrubbed and polished every
Saturday night for Sunday morning church; their
clothes always washed and starched and pressed
without one single crease anywhere; their food,
from cornmeal mush during the Depression to the
abundant holiday feasts later on. After we left
home we all still dropped by whenever we could
because you made your home a wonderful place to
be. Why did none of your children make that kind
of a home for you when you grew old and frail?

Because I never grew frail. At least not in
their mind. Your children will feel the
same about you.

You know, Grandma, you're right about that. You and I are strong and determined women — probably even willful! These things keep me moving in the direction I want to go.

Do you know how it will end for you?

No. Perhaps that is why I have come to this place. I want to determine the ending also. I want to die the way I lived, strong and with purpose. I don't want death to visit me like a fearsome stranger. I want to walk confidently into that final moment.

Just the way I did — heading out of that bathroom all on my own in spite of the warnings.

But it sounds so undignified. I want to be doing something noble, like protesting something or setting an example of great courage. You know, a story that can be retold with pride.

The circumstances of my death have made you ashamed of me?

No, of me.

So that is why you attempted to make me a villain, so you can then tell the story of my death without shame . . . as if I deserved my final moment?

Yes.

Then tell my story that way.

I did.

And what happened?

You were on the other side of the door when I called out.

So what have you decided is behind that door?

All the lies and doubts and misconceptions of my life.

What have you determined, then, is truth in my life?

I don't know.  Only you know.

That's correct.

I can only know for sure what I saw and heard and, most importantly, felt in my heart.

And what did you feel in your heart about me?

I loved you Grandma, in spite of all the devotion
you demanded of us and all your foolish accusations and silly notions. You were the most influen-
tial person in my life. I have your strength and
determination as well as your willful ways. Your
energy and perfection were an inspiration to me.
But you were very weak and wrong in your approach to men. I had to suffer a great deal to
change that within me because I took your notions
out into the world and made some serious mistakes, hurt some people who were entrusted to
my care. You did that part all wrong, Grandma.

But you recovered.

Yes, I did, because I worked so hard at it. I felt
there was something wonderful inside of me and all
around me, but I couldn't put it together, make it
work, unless I moved some of those attitudes out
of the way. So I guess I took the strength I got
from you and used it to work out the weakness I
also got from you.

That sounds like the way it should be.

It does, doesn't it? You can go now, Grandma. I
will be just fine.

But she didn't leave; she is with me still, and what a
wonderful feeling that is.

But the feeling grows slowly bittersweet. My heart begins to break. There is something I must do, please don't let it be too late. Grandpa, there are so many things I want to tell you.

I no longer want to hate you. I can remember so many good things now. You were a real craftsman and taught your sons how to work with wood, and paint, and do wiring, plumbing, barbering. Your daughters speak with fondness of the table, chairs and doll furniture you made for them as children. When I was a child, I used to sit and watch you work; fascinated by your technique and precision. And the family still uses the sausage press you fashioned out of an old Hoover vacuum cleaner.

> Those were good days for me. I'm glad you could find it in your heart to recall my accomplishments.

I wouldn't want to be remembered for only my mistakes and weaknesses.

> We all have them.

Yes, I know. When I could not forgive myself, I could not forgive you either. I think that refusing to forgive myself was really an act of denial and of pride. I wanted to be perfect and could not accept the fact I wasn't.

I know about perfection also.  When I
made drawers for a cabinet, even though
no one would see the inside corners, they
had to be so smooth they felt like one
piece of wood.

The things you made were absolutely beautiful,
without flaw.

Unlike me.

Unlike me too, Grandpa.  I guess we're alike in
many ways.  I also work my craft so that people
can glimpse the seamless perfection that runs
background to my own imperfect life.

Perfection.  Yes, life was so good.  I felt like
a rich man.  I was the head of a happy,
growing family,  the owner of a successful
business, a king!  Then in a flash the Depression took everything.  Everything
except Mama; she stayed by me, loved me,
respected me.

Yes, Grandpa, I know.  In her eyes you were still a
king!  I understand now what all that means.

## 20 - COMPASSION

With my jaws no longer clenched in bitterness and resentment, my lips were free to speak words of healing and salvation, for me.

Some acts are unforgivable. The people who commit them, however, must be remembered with charity of thought. It is possible their minds and hearts and lives were damaged beyond human repair.

The rock that was once my heart lay in pieces all around me. A richer, deeper love was now possible. My body, once cold and lifeless, now warmed with the excitement of what was next to be.

## 21 - LIFE ITSELF

I am filled with hope; on fire with the energy of love. Tell me, please, what now waits on the other side of that door? The door! It's gone! I can no longer see it's outline. Is this to become my forever?

The way out is up.

Oh, no you don't! I will have no more of that nonsense about a heaven up in the sky somewhere. Nothing is there that would be safe for a gentle person. Some things whirl around and explode. Others are sucked into black holes leading to even more vastness. "Up" is nowhere I'd want to be.

The way out is up.

Up where?

Up from the ground you stand on. Up from the shoes you put your feet into. Up from the bed you sleep on. Up from the chair you sit on. Up from the floor you pace back and forth over trying to figure out what will happen to you. You, you you!

I don't understand.

Listen.

I am listening! I've done everything I possibly can
— struggled with my faults and shortcomings; tried
to be honest with myself and with others; followed
the directions from within. I have done it all; there
is nothing more!

Then your search must be over.

Stop, I've had enough! Get away from me you
confounded nothingness! Yes, there *is* something
more. I never asked to be born, brought into an
existence from which there is no escape. I want a
say in all of this.

Sometimes as I drift into sleep, the reality of death
sweeps over me and I am terrified. At times when
I am relaxing in my warm and soothing bath, I am
stabbed by the thought of what waits for me at the
end of this . . . this what? This second? The next
second? Some future second? Panicked, I leap out
of my tub and begin to make plans — big giant
plans that will keep me so busy I won't notice
death. Or I write deep, mighty words, hoping one
of them will explain to me what is unexplainable. I
ask everyone I meet: Are *you* afraid to die? Do
you know anything for sure? Have you been given
any clues that might help me?

Out of all the brilliant minds that have passed through this plane of existence, not a one knew anything for sure.  Still I sit here like a fool, thinking it will be revealed to me.

> The answer is within.

Please leave me alone.  I am weary, sick of the struggle, there is nothing more I can do.

> What then is holding you here?

I can't say it; it's too silly, and too sad.

> Speak.

I don't want to die.  It's not fair!  There is nothing that could possibly make it all right for me to lose the people I love, the moments I cherish, the life I have worked so hard to make worthy.  And I have no choice but to live surrounded by forces I cannot stop or control — forces that will one day take all that I am.

> Yield when it comes.  Surrender.

Willingly?  Without a struggle?  How can I?  This life is all I have.

Learn humility. What you must give back
was not yours. In your busy days and
anxious nights, hold life above you, apart
from you. Know your place and live in
profound gratitude for the time you have.
Use it wisely in the pursuit of things beyond you. When the moment comes, let
go of those near and cup your hands. Fill
them with your final breath and take rest
for the work of your days will be complete.

The work of my days complete? Wait! The
words right here on this page are the work of my
days. Have you come for me? Is it my time to
go?

It is time for you to *let* go.

## 22 - THE RIDDLE

Let go, yes.  But I don't know how.  There is still so
much I want to hold on to.  Please help me.

The connections in life, do you feel them?

Yes, they come sometimes as coincidence, sometimes as miracle, sometimes as explosions of insight.
Yes, I feel the connections.

Follow them.  They are the web of life: the
strands that held your trunk to the floor, the
strands that circled your heart at Brandt's,
the strands that kept your life together when
it seemed to fall apart, the shimmering
strands that lured you through the door to
this place.  The door exists no more because
you have faced your fears and your lies and
are now ready to return to life.

Can I have a little more time?

You have asked all the questions.  You have
tested all the theories.  You have drawn the
only conclusions wisdom will allow.  What
remains?

To feel love.  Love so powerful it removes all sadness.  Love so gentle it eases all pain.  Love deeper
than anything I have ever felt or could imagine.

It does not exist beyond you. You are that love. If you have bestowed it without condition, if you have received it without merit, you have experienced all there is to love.

I know what you say is true. The more I feel this communion with others, the more my life fills with wonder and joy — the courage to go on; the humility to let go.

You are endowed with something no other form of life has. You can choose to love. There is nothing more powerful, more splendid, more eternal.

It is time now for you to leave. Answer please the riddle: What is Life?

Life is part of the Mystery — the Mystery that has no words, no parts, no rhyme or reason; the Mystery that stands before us, behind us, within us; the Mystery that reveals its presence in our life through Love.

Give this Mystery no name — for to name it is to limit it. Give it no definition — for to define it is to own it. Stand before it in awe. Surrender when it calls. Trust that which can be known only in the signs around you: life, death, more life. Participate to the fullest with compassion, the glory of your humanity. And in your wisdom, think not that you are God.

# CONCLUSION

What did I actually accomplish as I sat here each morning before the dawn broke, fevered with the search for truth?  Somewhere inside of me, I already knew all the answers.  What happened, however, is that I put them down on paper, like a contract, which I then began to honor with my life.

I refused daydreams that did not come from the reality of my life and its people.

I bought nothing I did not need.  And I assessed each need carefully, with new guidelines.

I grew more generous.  Fought the urge to grab, hoard, and hide.  Began giving away my "treasures."

I approached food more reverently.  Shopped for things that feed hunger rather than desire.  Mindful of the hunger in others, I blessed the tiniest morsel and ate it in gratitude.

I learned to welcome sleep.  Grew less afraid of the dark.  Prayed for the poor souls within it.

I faced painful moments of the past and did not crumble, but gained wisdom, strength, and compassion.

I let go of the anger carried for most of my life. Uncovered hurts and let them be healed.

I accepted my place and time on this earth. Began the preparation, emotionally, to let go when it is time.

And I focused my life on the only reality there is: this moment.

"What lies beyond?" The answer matters less and less each day as I grow in my capacity and ability to love. Some day I will be gone. If there is nothing more, the memories of my life will be enough to carry me across the threshold and into the endless forever of the question.

## Also by Barbara Ritter Garrison

Precious Jewel Person
Reflections on the Spirituality of Everyday Life

141 pages, $8.95
ISBN: 0-914070-99-1

Available at most Christian bookstores or from
ACTA Publications, 4848 N. Clark Street,
Chicago, Illinois 60640.
(800) 397-2282